Classical Chinese Gardens

Foreign Languages Press Beijing

"Culture of China" Editorial Board:

Consultants: Cai Mingzhao, Zhao Changqian, Huang Youyi and Liu Zhibin
Chief Editor: Xiao Xiaoming
Board Members: Xiao Xiaoming, Li Zhenguo, Tian Hui, Hu Baomin,
Fang Yongming, Hu Kaimin, Cui Lili and Lan Peijin

Text by: Yao Tianxing, Gu Yuan
Photographers: Yao Tianxing, Zhou Rende, Sun Shuming, Chen Keyin,
Dong Ruicheng, Zhu Jie, Yan Xiangqun, Zhang Keqing,
Liu Jiwen, Xu Tingchang, Lin Jianhua, Xie Xinfa, Bai Ping,
Sun Baohua, Lan Peijin, Yu Zhiyong, Du Dianwen
Translators: Kuang Peihua, Ouyang Weiping, Wang Qin
English Editor: Yu Ling
Designers: An Lijian, Yuan Qing
Managing Editor: Lan Peijin

First Edition 2003

Classical Chinese Gardens

ISBN 7-119-03183-X

© Foreign Languages Press
Published by Foreign Languages Press
24 Baiwanzhuang Road, Beijing 100037, China
Home Page: http://www.flp.com.cn
E-mail Addresses: info@flp.com.cn
sales@flp.com.cn
Distributed by China International Book Trading Corporation
35 Chegongzhuang Xilu, Beijing 100044, China
P.O.Box 399, Beijing, China

Printed in the People's Republic of China

Classical Chinese Gardens

Foreword

In the long history of Chinese civilization, many scholars have left beautiful poems describing exquisite classical Chinese gardens, including those of the emperor's temporary residences, rich families' flower gardens, or lofty imperial palaces. Today, when we pay visits to these gardens to appreciate the elegant halls, towers, pavilions and corridors, we can still feel the luxury and poeticism of the owners of these gardens, and cannot help feeling: "Though man-made, these gardens are so natural."

With their long history and consummate art, classical Chinese gardens occupy an important position in the world history of gardens. Hence, China enjoys the reputation of being the mother of garden construction. As both a material and spiritual expression of the most direct and closest connection between man and nature, classical Chinese gardens are an artistic combination of ancient architecture and horticultural design, as well as a component of traditional Chinese culture. Now, many classical gardens have been named as key historical monuments under state protection, of which many are included on the UNESCO World Heritage List.

Classical Chinese gardens, which are located all over the country, fall into three main types—imperial, private, and temple gardens. Imperial gardens generally refer to those in which the emperors administered state affairs, enjoyed entertainment, and lived, with large-scale architecture, luxurious decoration and bright colors, like an imperial palace. Such examples include the Summer Palace, Yuanmingyuan (the Old Summer Palace), and the Mountain Resort in Chengde. Usually, imperial gardens have natural hills and water; their general layout is based on natural scenery and private gardens. Many imperial gardens contain the exquisite and enchanting characteristics of the gardens south of the Yangtze River. Private gardens are closely related to civilian residential houses; they were privately owned by

bureaucrats, landlords, rich merchants, and the scholar-gentry. They are the further extension and expansion of living spaces. Small in size, a private garden is a place for the owners to rest, entertain friends, hold banquets, or read. Most private gardens are in Jiangsu and Zhejiang provinces. There is an old saying: "Hangzhou is famous for its lakes and hills; Yangzhou for its gardens and pavilions; Suzhou for its shops." Temple gardens, in various sizes, are mostly located in beautiful environments with natural hills and water. They are attached to Buddhist and Taoist temples, altars, or shrines. In the shape of a courtyard, the temple garden often contains lush green trees with small bridges and running water—an ideal place for scholars to cultivate their minds. Here we will give a brief introduction to some imperial, private, and temple gardens.

With a history of over 3,000 years of garden construction, China has perfected the art of garden construction. Tracing back the footsteps of our ancestors, we find that natural landscapes and large-scale construction were a virtually universal manifestation of the high position of emperors, princes, generals, ministers, and high officials. Inscriptions on bones and tortoise shells of the Shang Dynasty (c. 16th - 11th century B.C.) describe ancient Chinese pleasure grounds near mountains, rivers, woods and other places abundant in birds and animals. In the Qin (221 - 206 B.C.) and Han (206 B.C. - 220 A.D.) dynasties, the places specially designed for emperors' entertainment were called 苑 (meaning garden). Emperor Qin Shihuang (r. 221 - 210 B.C.) had Shanglin Garden constructed to the south of the Weishui River, including the Efang Palace. Historical records reveal: "The Efang Palace was about 400 m from east to west and nearly 150 m from south to north, and it could hold 10,000 people." Emperor Wudi (r. 140 - 87 B.C.) of the Han Dynasty had Shanglin Garden expanded and constructed Taiye Pool as well as Penglai, Fangzhang and Yingzhou hills. Many others popularly adopted the layout of "one pool and three hills" later. After the Han Dynasty, Chinese society was in turbulence, and many officials and scholars felt disheartened. They withdrew from society and lived in solitude, writing and painting landscapes to vent their feelings. All of a sudden, many landscape gardens seeking harmony between man and nature sprang up like mushrooms. During the reign of Emperor Mingdi (r. 58 - 75 A.D.) of the Eastern Han Dynasty, China's first Buddhist temple was established in Luoyang, which gave rise to the birth of temple gardens and added the customs of Buddhist temple construction to other types of ancient gardens, especially imperial gardens. During the Wei, Jin, and Southern and Northern dynasties (220-581), Buddhism and Taoism flourished throughout China. As an integral part of religious architecture, many temple gardens were constructed, reflecting the profound aesthetic and ideo-logical trends of the era. Increasing numbers of people sought gardens pleasing to both the eye and mind. In the Tang Dy-nasty (618 - 907), landscape gardens developed on all fronts because of the country's advanced economy, strong state power, and flourishing culture. Many large-scale imperial gardens inside and outside the capital of Chang'an were constructed, such as Forbidden Garden, Eastern and Western Internal Gardens, Southern Gardens, Taiye Pool, and Penglai Hill. In the Song Dynasty (960 - 1279) the construction of private gardens came into vogue. From the capital to the countryside, from the emperors to officials and ordinary people, all vied with each other in building private gardens. As scholars occupied all the state administrative positions during the Song Dynasty, private gardens constructed by scholars became very common.

After the Liao Dynasty (947 - 1125), the emperors of the Jin (1115 - 1234), Yuan (1271 - 1368), Ming (1368 - 1644)

and especially Qing (1644 - 1911) dynasties constructed large-scale imperial gardens in Beijing. According to historical records, almost all the emperors of various dynasties preferred handling state affairs in imperial gardens, especially the emperors of the Qing Dynasty. Thanks to development over 2,000 years and so, Chinese classical garden construction art matured in terms of outlay, construction techniques, breeding of birds and animals, and cultivation of flowers and trees. By fully using the natural landscape and preexisting favorable conditions, and absorbing the excellent traditions of the gardens of the Tang and Song dynasties, garden construction art reached a historical height. In addition, the economy of the Ming and Qing dynasties developed and expanded, leading to a bountiful national treasury. All this provided material and technical conditions for the construction of gardens. The Qing Dynasty took the lead in the number and variety of gardens of all the dynasties in the Chinese history. As a result a great number of large-scale imperial gardens were built, such as Yuanmingyuan, Quiet and Pleas-ant Garden (Fragrant Hill), the Summer Palace, and Beihai Park. In the imperial garden the emperor could both attend to state affairs and relax. Hence the imperial garden was more lively than the solemn and magnificent imperial palace.

The imperial gardens and the gardens of the princes' residences display the highest achievements of the garden construction art. During the reign of Emperor Kangxi (r. 1662-1722), the construction of large-scale imperial gardens was concentrated in the northwestern suburbs of Beijing as well as Chengde in Hebei Province. In the 42nd year of the Kangxi reign period (1703), the construction of the Mountain Resort started at Chengde. The site was providently endowed with a picture-perfect landscape and a cool and pleasant climate. In the mountain resort, the emperor and all the members of the imperial family could enjoy themselves by practicing martial arts and hunting. From 1703 to 1790, 72 scenic attractions in the Mountain Resort were completed, covering an area of about 533 hectares, divided into three scenic categories—lakes, plains and mountains. The mountains are not tall, the lakes are not large, and the islands are crisscrossed, full of changes. The complexes of buildings are scattered here and there, hidden among mountain forests. In its heyday the Mountain Resort boasted 72 scenic spots, 36 of which were constructed during the Kangxi reign, and the remaining 36 in the Qianlong reign. Each scenic spot changes with the season, and each is named after a mountain, river, forest, or spring. The Mountain Resort of Chengde gathers all the characteristics of the architectural outlay of north China, integrates the construction art styles of various regions in China, and ingeniously combines the simple and unsophisticated characteristics of architecture of north China with the graceful and exquisite decoration techniques of south China. The Eight Outlying Temples refers to a group of monastic complexes situated outside the Mountain Resort of Chengde. Together with the imperial resort, the complex is a distillation of the aesthetic trends of the Qing Dynasty.

The imperial garden complexes of northwestern Beijing are crossed by sparkling streams, studded with glistening springs, and set against the backdrop of a jumble of mountains. During the height of the Qing Dynasty, many large-scale famous imperial gardens were constructed there. None of the Western Hills imperial gardens are better known than the "Three Hills and Five Gardens," which refer to Xiangshan (Fragrant Hill), Yuquan (Jade Spring) and Wanshou (Longevity) Hills, and Jingyiyuan (Garden of Quiet Pleasure) in Xiangshan Park, Jingmingyuan (Garden of Quiet Brightness) on Yuquan Hill, Qingyiyuan (Garden of Rippling Waves) on Wanshou Hill, Changchunyuan (Garden of Pleas-

ant Spring), and Yuanmingyuan (Garden of Perfect Brightness or the Old Summer Palace), thus forming the largest imperial garden area. The oldest imperial garden was Changchunyuan, which was constructed by Emperor Kangxi. To the northwest was a private garden built in the Ming Dynasty; Emperor Yongzheng renovated that garden and named it Yuanmingyuan. Yongzheng liked to enjoy himself there and handle state matters away from the turmoil of the world. Yuanmingyuan was the most magnificent imperial garden in Chinese history. Several emperors of the Qing Dynasty, including Yongzheng, Qianlong, Jiaqing, and Daoguang, spent tremendous national strength and financial resources for its expansion and renovation. With an area of about 347 hectares, of which half was taken up by water, Yuanmingyuan had a total constructed area of 150,000 square meters. Besides garden architecture, Yuanmingyuan contained more than 150 other attractions, such as altars, temples, theaters, and libraries. A museum of garden construction and horticulture, Yuanmingyuan contained imitations of many famous scenic spots throughout the country. Thanks to its large scale, varied scenery, and consummate achievements, Yuanmingyuan enjoyed the prestige of being the "Garden Surpassing All Gardens."

The world-famous garden now lies in ruins. Only a few stone ruins remain, along with some desolate scenery. We may, however, take a tour of a well-preserved imperial garden—the Summer Palace. While walking in the Summer Palace, you may imagine you are following the footsteps of the emperors of ancient China. The predecessor of the current Summer Palace was Qingyiyuan, constructed in the 15th year of the Qianlong reign period (1750) after the completion of the scenic spots of Yuanmingyuan to celebrate his mother's birthday and with the pretext of controlling the river. The construction of Qingyiyuan lasted more than 10 years. Due to the natural beauty of its lakes and hills, Qingyiyuan enjoyed a high reputation among all imperial gardens. The Summer Palace can be divided into two major parts—the front hill and lake, and the rear hill and lake, with a total area of nearly 300 hectares, of which three fourths is taken by water. The Summer Palace includes over 3,000 ancient architectural structures, which cover an area of 70,000 square meters. On the basis of the natural hills and lakes, this imperial garden includes numerous classical structures, such as corridors, bridges, pavilions, water-side pavilions, halls, temples, and terraces, many of which are replicas of scenic spots and historical sites in southeast China. An old saying goes: "Which is the pleasantest place in the Yanshan Mountains? It is the park by the Kunming Lake (i.e., the Summer Palace)."

In the 10th year of the Xianfeng reign period (1860), Qingyiyuan, Yuanmingyuan, and the other imperial gardens were sacked during the invasion of Anglo-French allied forces. The buildings were burned to the ground and the treasures and cultural relics in them were looted. In the 12th year of the Guangxu reign (1886), Empress Dowager Cixi diverted a large amount of silver from the navy's allocation to rebuild the garden on the ruins of Qingyiyuan, renaming it Yiheyuan (known as the Summer Palace), meaning "Garden of Health and Peace," in 1888, which presents the magnificence and elegance of the former Qingyiyuan. Now, the Summer Palace is the best-preserved imperial garden in China. Because of limited financial resources, Yuanmingyuan was not restored. Now people can only imagine the formerly majestic Yuanmingyuan from the ruined lakes, stones, and foundations in the park.

If imperial gardens are majestic and imposing, with large halls and temples, private gardens are small and elegant, with pavilions and bridges scattered here and there. When hearing rain falling onto palm leaves, watching the sunshine on moving bamboo grooves, and enjoying exquisite and beautifully shaped rocks from Lake Tai, the observer feels carefree and joyous. The beauty of a natural landscape is condensed and reproduced in a small space. Private gardens reached their zenith during the Ming and Qing dynasties, and were spread all over the country. Many private gardens of high artistic value are located in the cities to the south of the Yangtze River, where the economy was prosperous and a large number of talented people were concentrated. Some excellent examples are Mountain Villa with Embracing Beauty, Lion Grove, the Humble Administrator's Garden, and the Lingering Garden in Suzhou and Geyuan and Heyuan gardens in Yangzhou, representing the historical peak of the development of the garden in feudal society. The Humble Administrator's Garden includes halls, terraces, towers, pavilions, balustrades and corridors. One views new scenery with each step forward. Shihu Garden features condensed scenery and winding paths that lead to quiet and secluded spots, away from the turmoil of the world. The Surging Waves Pavilion is a fine example showing how the natural landscape both inside and outside can be integrated. In the Lingering Garden, hills, water surfaces, trees and flowers combine to form a garden of multiple depths. Size and height, straight lines and curves, shade and light—all these are alternated to bring about a spatial system of varying hues and contrasts. Therefore, it is an important contribution of private gardens to garden construction techniques and ideology. With the limited space of a garden, nature is fastidiously imitated. Private gardens, small in size, are elegant and tasteful, perform multiple functions and can be combined with the natural scenery.

During the Qing Dynasty, Yangzhou became a communications hub and a collection and distribution center of salt.

Its advanced economy and culture provided the material and intellectual encouragement for garden construction. During the reign of Emperor Qianlong, the private gardens of Yangzhou enjoyed a high reputation—"Yangzhou has the best gardens in the world"—because of their large number and beauty. Yangzhou was also one of the major foreign trade cities at that time. Through extensive commercial exchanges between Chinese and foreign merchants, Western garden construction techniques were introduced to the private gardens in Yangzhou. As a result, a large number of private gardens of different styles sprang up in the city. Walking along the Slender West Lake, visitors can find row upon row of villas, gardens and buildings erected on the lakeside, each having its own unique shape and beauty. A poem goes: "The lake is flanked by flowers and willow trees, and the road to the hill is lined by towers and terraces." Today, Yangzhou still has more than 30 private gardens, including Geyuan Garden, Craggy Stone Mountain Lodge, Jixiao Villa, Yuyuan Garden, Xiaopangu, and Weiyou Garden.

A popular saying goes: "Above, they have Paradise. Here, we have Suzhou and Hangzhou." Suzhou and Hangzhou are lands of abundance and prosperity. Besides their natural scenery, these two cities are known for their breathtaking gardens. On the basis of highly mature rural construction in south Jiangsu Province, private gardens were constructed, in which architecture and natural scenery had a symbiotic relationship, mutually enhancing each other's radiance and beauty and forming a perfect whole. In the limited space of a private garden, visitors may enjoy natural scenery that is more concentrated and representative than nature itself. During the Taiping Heavenly Kingdom rebellion, the gardens of Suzhou were badly damaged. It was not until late in the Qing Dynasty that garden construction revived, when bureaucrats and warlords vied with each other in displays of conspicuous consumption. In the 1950s, 188 well-preserved residences remained in Suzhou. Gardens in Suzhou are picturesque, full of the flavors of history and culture.

Hangzhou is also one of the cities in southeast China with a large number of private gardens. The charming scenery around the West Lake was highly praised in numerous poems and other writings by ancient scholars. The two chain-like dykes across West Lake, which contribute to the graceful scenery, have been imitated time and again in other gardens. For instance, when Emperor Qianlong had Qingyiyuan built, Kunming Lake was modeled after West Lake, including its temples, bridges and dykes.

In examining the history of China's classical gardens, a certain cultural spirit has always been present. More specifically, it is not a unitary cultural spirit. The different aesthetic perceptions of imperial, monastic and private gardens originated in different cultural spirits. Without such spirits, the architecture, flowers, trees, and landscape construction are only special techniques. The influence of China's rich ideological and cultural heritage on garden construction techniques is an important reason why China's classical gardens have their own unique characteristics. Chinese classical garden art embodies the national culture in a nutshell, including almost all categories of ancient sciences and culture. It originated from nature, but is higher than the poetic beauty of nature, and is based on the combination of natural and artificial. All these reflect their value as a world cultural heritage in history and art. Among the world's gardens, Chinese gardens, as an independent garden system, enjoy a high reputation.

CONTENTS

The Summer Palace

(Yiheyuan 颐和园)

The Summer Palace in northwest Beijing is the most complete of China's surviving imperial gardens, featuring a magnificent group of ancient buildings in natural scenery dominated by Longevity Hill (Wanshoushan) and Kunming Lake. Housed among magnificent pavilions, bridges, corridors, halls and palaces with over 3,000 rooms, the Summer Palace has enjoyed a reputation as "the First Garden in the Divine Land" since the early Yuan (1271-1368) and Ming dynasties (1368-1644). In 1860, this magnificent imperial garden—along with the nearby Yuanmingyuan (Old Summer Palace) —was plundered and burned to the ground by Anglo-French allied forces. In 1886, it was reconstructed under the orders of Empress Dowager Ci Xi with funds that had been earmarked for the Chinese Navy. In 1900, the Summer Palace was again destroyed by the Eight-Power (Austria, Britain, France, Germany, Italy, Japan, Tsarist Russia and the United States) Allied Forces. It was restored in 1903, so that the resplendent buildings—including the Pagoda of Buddhist Incense, the Cloud-dispelling Hall and the Great Stage in the Garden of Virtuous Harmony—are in a style of wood construction characteristic of the Qing Dynasty (1644-1911).

At the southern foot of Longevity Hill, the Long Corridor winds along the lake for 728-meters, making it the longest of China's ancient corridors. At the eastern foot of Longevity Hill lies the Garden of Harmonious Delights, "a garden within a garden" that is an imitation of the Garden for Ease of Mind at the foot of the Huishan Hill in the city of Wuxi. Most pavilions, bridges, corridors, halls and palaces that make up the Summer Palace are reminiscent of scenic spots and historical sites south of the Yangtze River, in landscaping that recreates natural settings. On December 2,1998, the Summer Palace was added to the list of World Cultural Heritage sites.

A view along the western slope of Longevity Hill. The Summer Palace, epitomizing the best of Chinese gardening art, attracts tourists from all over the world.

The Pagoda of Buddhist Incense

The Long Corridor

A distant view of the West Causeway

A bird's-eye view of the 17-arch Bridge

The West Causeway in snow

The Garden of Harmonious Delights in summer

The Bronze Ox

The Great Stage in the
Garden of Virtuous Har-
mony

The Willow Bridge

The Suzhou Street

The Old Summer Palace
(Ruins of Yuanmingyuan 圆明园)

First built in the Liao Dynasty (947-1125), the Old Summer Palace was completed in the Ming and Qing dynasties to become an imperial garden of nearly indescribable magnificence, covering an area of 350 hectares (1 hectare=2.47 acres) –half of it water–that included three separate gardens: the Garden of Perfection and Brightness, the Garden of Everlasting Spring and the Garden of Superb Spring. Many scenic sites in Old Summer Palace were reproductions of famous gardens including Hangzhou's West Lake with its 10 scenic sites. One area of the Old Summer Palace was devoted to European-style mansions, known as the Western Buildings, which furnished the first and only instance in the world of Eastern and Western architectural styles grouped together. In its harmonious use of gardening arts from North and South China and its combination of Chinese and Western culture, the Old Summer Palace represented China's gardening art at its highest level. Along with the nearby Summer Palace, this treasure of architectural and landscape design was destroyed in 1860 by the Anglo-French allied forces and again in 1900 by the Eight-Power Allied Forces. Today part of the original 350 hectares is open as a public park for boating, strolling and viewing what little remains of the architecture, including broken stone pillars and collapsed arches from the Western-style buildings. A museum in the park chronicles the garden's history.

A courtyard on the western island in the Blessing Lake

A stream in autumn

The Bridge of Reading-Your-Mind in the Garden of Preferring Spring

The ruins of the
Lion Grove

The residential palace of the Qing emperors in "Clear Sky over Nine Prefectures"

"Jasper Terrace on Penglai Island" in the center of Blessing Lake. During the reign of Emperor Qianlong, the Empress Dowager was invited here every year to watch the dragon boat race at the Dragon Boat Festival. (Portrayed by court painters of the Qing Dynasty)

The ruins of the
Western Buildings

The Green-Mirroring Pavilion

20

"Taoist Wonderland," representative of the architectural style found at the Old Summer Palace

North Sea Park
(Beihai Park 北海公园)

Built in the Liao Dynasty (947-1125), Beihai Park in Beijing is one of the best examples of China's classical gardens, featuring a lake, artificial hills, pavilions, halls, temples and covered corridors. The park area covers 68 hectares, more than half of which is the North [Sea] Lake. The park was rebuilt several times throughout the Jin, Yuan, Ming and Qing– altogether five dynasties. When Kublai Khan of the Yuan Dynasty (1271-1368) captured Beijing, almost everything in the capital was destroyed except the area of Beihai where a main hall was rebuilt as the imperial court. The White Dagoba, the white shrine pagoda in Tibetan style that dominates the park, was built in honor of the fifth Dalai Lama when he visited Beijing in 1651. The Dagoba, the Temple of Eternal Peace, Hall of Law Wheel, Hall of Universal Peace, and Hall of Rippling Water along with covered corridors similar to the one at the Summer Palace are situated on Jade Island in the center of the lake, connected to land by bridges on the south and the east. Other scenic areas lie around the lake including the Hall of Receiving Light–the main structure of the park–in Round Town, which is enclosed by a wall five meters high. Among the treasures in Round Town are a jade urn said to have been used as a wine vessel by Kublai Khan. Ancient pines grow here as well.

The Jade Islet, the White Dagoba

The

on Pavilion   The Nine-dragon Screen   The Tray of Holding Dew

The Studio of Peaceful Mind

The Round Town

The Jade Buddha in the Hall
of Receiving Lights

Fragrant Hill
(*Xiangshan* 香山)

Fragrant Hill in the Western Hills of Beijing features clear spring waters, forests, and winding streams that meander through 150 hectares of pavilions, towers and terraces in what was once an imperial game and hunting reserve, and later in 1745 an imperial park. The park was destroyed by foreign troops in 1860 and 1900 (See also the Summer Palace and the Old Summer Palace). Fragrant Hill becomes a major tourist attraction in the fall when the red leaves of the smoke trees–planted during the reign of Qing Emperor Qianlong–turn the hill a blazing red. The normal tour route starts at the east gate with access to the Luminous Temple, a Tibetan-style monastery built in 1780 as a residence for the Sixth Panchen Lama, as well as the Glazed-Tile Pagoda. The three main paths on Fragrant Hill feature other pagodas, temples and pavilions. The Hall of Deep Reflection has a lotus pond in the center surrounded by covered corridors and connecting halls, which is an example of southern Chinese structures in a northern Chinese garden.

The Glazed-Tile Pagoda

The Chamber of Deep Reflection

The Chamber of Listening to
the Whispering Snow

The Garden of Viewing Pleasures

The Pavilion Facing the Waterfall

Autumn at the Double Purity Pavilion

Snow on Fragrant Hill

27

Coal Hill Park
(Jingshan Park 景山公园)

Jingshan Park (used to be called Coal Hill Park), just opposite the north gate of the Forbidden City in Beijing, offers one of the best panoramic views of the Palace Museum and of the whole city. Enclosed by a stately red wall, the 47.5-meter-high hill that makes up Jingshan Park was created from earth excavated from the Beihai Park area in the early Ming Dynasty. In the Yuan Dynasty, the hill evolved into an imperial garden with pine and fruit trees. To the northeast of the hill, is a complex of buildings typical of the Qing style, including the Hall of Imperial Longevity where the imperial family displayed their ancestor's portraits, now a children's palace. A pavilion stands on each of the five peaks of Jingshan Park, and the view from the middle pavilion is the best.

The Beautiful View Pavilion

Jingshan Park situated to the north of the Forbidden City (the Palace Museum)

Outside the Hall of Imperial Longevity

Jingshan at sunset

Prince Gong's Garden
(*Gongwangfu* 恭王府)

Prince Gong's Garden, the best-preserved private garden in Beijing, features two particularly attractive buildings: the Xijin Chamber made from precious rosewood and chinaberry, and a red building with a length of 160 meters that spans the estate, making it the longest building of families connected to the royal court in Beijing. The garden was granted to Prince Gong during the reign of Qing Emperor Xianfeng (1851-1860), and reconstructed according to the description of a garden in the Chinese classical novel, A Dream of Red Mansions. Water was introduced into the garden and corridors and waterside pavilions were built. Covering 2.5 hectares, Prince Gong's Garden includes 31 garden structures.

The Great Stage

The Mid-Lake Pavilion

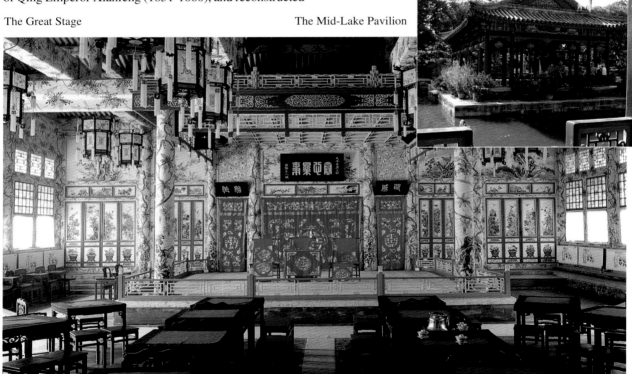

The corridor

"The Hill of Solitary Delight" rockwork

The only door of Western style in
Chinese classical gardens outside the
Old Summer Palace

31

The Banana Courtyard

Artificial hills shade the buildings-
-the Dripping Green Rock

The Bat Pool and the Bat Hall (In Chinese, the characters for "bat" and "blessing" are homonyms.)

The front door of the Summer Resort

Mountain Resort
(Bishu Shanzhuang 避暑山庄)

Situated in the north of the city of Chengde in Hebei Province, the Mountain Resort has the largest area—564 hectares—of any imperial garden still existing in China. Construction began in 1703 in the Qing Dynasty and was completed in 1790 during the reign of Emperor Qianlong who, following his grandfather Emperor Kangxi, gave names to and wrote poems for 36 scenic sites at the Mountain Resort. Surrounded by a 10-kilometer-long stone wall, the Mountain Resort includes a palace area, garden area and mountain area. The palace area is divided into different water areas by small islands, causeways and bridges in a way that creates an atmosphere similar to that found south of the Yangtze River. On the north, a triangular garden area features over 100 towers, halls, pavilions and terraces and 72 scattered scenic sites. The mountain area—undulating, tree-covered hills—makes up two-thirds of the garden. In its natural setting, the Mountain Resort incorporates both northern and southern gardening styles in a way that displays both the overall majesty of an imperial garden as well as the look of gardens south of the Yangtze River.

A view of the simple and fine complex of palaces

Inside the Hall of Austerity and Sincerity

A distant view of the Mountain Resort

The "Golden Hill" modeled on a temple of the same name in Zhenjiang City

Waterside pavilions

Undulating hills in the west of the Mountain Resort

The Tower of Misty Rain

A distant view of the Club Peak from the northern wall of the Summer Resort

Shihu Garden
(*Shihuyuan* 十笏园）

Built in 1885 in the Qing Dynasty, this private garden in Weifang City on the Shangdong Peninsula was created on the site of the former residence of Hu Bangzuo, a Ming Dynasty vice-minister of the Ministry of Justice. The garden is named Shihu (ten *hu*) because it is only 0.2 of a hectare, or as small as ten *hu*, which is a tablet officials held to note down orders when receiving an audience with the emperor. Shihu Garden has features typical of gardens found in northern China, with grand rockworks and a pool. On the axis of the garden opposite Shihu Thatched Abode stands Yanxiang (Fragrant Inkstone) Tower that offers a panoramic view of the garden. The garden has simple architecture with colors richer than those in gardens south of the Yangtze River.

Principal view

Decorative wall

37

Heyuan Garden
(*Heyuan* 何园)

The Heyuan Garden was built along the north bank of the ancient canal in Yangzhou, Jiangsu Province, in 1875 with a residential area in the south and a garden in the north. The garden is the most beautiful part with a winding pool, artificial hills and bridges that cross the water. A feature of Heyuan Garden is that its corridors, paths and streams wind through the whole garden, forming upper and lower levels, the only example of this among gardens south of the Yangtze River.

To save space, the hill was built against the wall.

The entrance to "the Jixiao Villa"

The Boat Hall

Decorative wall and the
Moon Gate

39

A corner of the eastern garden

The Mid-Water Pavilion

Light through space between stones reflects on the water, forming "a man-made moon."

Monk Shitao, a famous landscape painter, is said to have written the name of lodge.

Craggy Stone Mountain Lodge
(*Pianshi Shanfang* 片石山房)

Craggy Stone Mountain Lodge in Yangzhou was the villa of Wu Jialong, an Anhui native, during the reign of Qing Emperor Qianlong (1736-1796). Although it is only 780 square meters in area, the villa appears delicate and refined with meandering streams and connecting corridors among pavilions. It now is part of the He Garden. To the south of a winding pool stand three waterside pavilions in the face of an artificial hill. In the east of the garden there is a *nanmu* (a kind of hardwood) hall built in late Ming Dynasty. The inscription of nine poems written by Shitao (a Qing Dynasty monk and landscape painter) on the east wall is considered of high aesthetical value.

The Waterside Pavilion and the Study with Half Wall

Entrances in the shapes of crescent, vase and lantern

Bright Moonlit Tower

(*Erfen Mingyue Lou* 二分明月楼)

Situated at the south end of the Guangling Street in Yangzhou, this building was built by a wealthy Yuan family. Its essence is captured in this poem written in the Tang Dynasty (618-907) by Xu Ning: "When the full moon shines all over the world, it favors Yangzhou the most."

The Garden of Family Wang
(*Wangshi Xiaoyuan* 汪氏小苑)

Located at Diguandi of Dongquanmen in Yangzhou, the Garden of Family Wang is one of the complete existing private gardens of salt merchants from the late Qing Dynasty. With almost 100 old houses still standing, its residences and gardens are well integrated into three exquisite gardens—"Keqidi" (A Place Where You Can Enjoy a Long Stay), "Xiaoyuan Chunshen" (A Small Garden in Deep Spring) and "Yingxi" (Welcoming the Morning Sun).

Brick carving on a shrine

"Xiaoyuan Chunshen" (A Small Garden in Deep Spring) at the northeast corner of the garden

The alley formed by fire-proof walls

44

可軒棲

"Keqidi" (A Place Where You Can Enjoy a Long
Stay) at the southwest corner of the garden

The well-arranged residence and garden

The Hall of Spring Sunshine was delicately decorated.

Pearl Garden
(*Zhenyuan* 珍园)

Situated in the Pearl Garden Hotel in downtown Yangzhou, the small but delicately arranged Pearl Garden was built by a salt merchant Li Xizhen in the late Qing Dynasty. The two surviving scenic spots are a waterside pavilion in the southeast of the garden and a pavilion with fancy windows, winding corridor and an artificial hill in the west of the garden. At the southeast corner of the garden are a lake and artificial hills in which there is a cave with ascending stairs.

Geyuan Garden
(*Geyuan* 个园)

Geyuan Garden was built toward the mid-19th century in the Qing Dynasty by a salt merchant Huang Yingtai in Yangzhou. The garden features bamboo and various kinds of unusual rockery arrangements in bamboo-and-rock scenery unique to China, and especially outstanding in the Geyuan Garden. Within the garden, thousands of bamboo trees are so densely planted that they make up a forest. The builder adopted a technique of classical garden construction art—"using rocks for different hills"—to create rockery scenes representing the four seasons: Taihu Lake rocks for summer, yellow stones for autumn, jade-like stones for winter, and green bamboo and stalagmites for spring. This is the only example of such an arrangement in existing classical gardens in China.

Bamboo and rocks are a feature of Geyuan Garden.

Spring landscape

Jade-like stones create a winter landscape.

Yellow stones for autumn

Taihu Lake rocks for summer

A lattice window

Rolling Stone Dreamland
(*Juanshi Dongtian* 卷石洞天)

One of the 24 Scenic Spots of Yangzhou in the Qing Dynasty, Rolling Stone Dreamland has been restored in recent years to become the first scenic spot in the Slender West Lake Scenic Area. The "Rolling Stone" refers to the garden's fist-sized stones. Lake rocks are not available in Yangzhou so the rockeries in the garden are crafted of small stones. The garden is composed of three parts: water courtyard in the east, rockery courtyard in the middle and land courtyard in the northeast.

Pictures show the scenery between the water courtyard and rockery courtyard.

Winding Stream in the West Garden
(*Xiyuan Qushui*西园曲水)

Also one of the 24 Scenic Areas of Yangzhou, Winding Stream in the West Garden was built in 1765 in the Qing Dynasty. A tree-lined stream twists and winds westward from the Rolling Stone Dreamland to a hill, making it possible to visit by boat. A long corridor by the stream is an outstanding feature of the garden.

The Bonsai Garden on the lawn in front of West Corridor and Yuanxiang (Fragrant Courtyard) Pavilion

The Slender West Lake Garden
(*Shouxihu* 瘦西湖)

The Slender West Lake Garden is one of the best known gardens in China that are situated around lakes. Located in the northwest of Yangzhou, the Slender West Lake Garden has scenery that rivals that of the West Lake in Hangzhou. Originally a city moat that served as a flood-relief channel of Yangzhou starting in the Sui and Tang dynasties for over 1,000 years, Slender West Lake was constructed through several dynasties as a well-known resort area of classical gardens. Li Bai, the Tang Dynasty poet, once wrote, "I departed from my old friend at the Yellow Crane Tower; he will go to Yangzhou in the misty month of flowers." The 24 Scenic Areas of Slender West Lake Garden were created along almost all of the ten-*li* banks of the lake between 1751 and 1765. But later, the 24 Scenic Areas became mostly deserted, and it was not until 1949 that most of the landscape as seen today was restored.

Fishing Dais

Spring willows on the long dyke

Entrence to "Small Golden Hill"

Xuyuan Garden

Yueguan (Appreciating the Moon) Hall with precious furniture of the Ming and Qing dynasties

Five-Pavilion
Bridge and White
Pagoda

Courtyard in front
of Musical Instru-
ment Chamber

Fu (Mallard) House

A path by the water leads northward to Pingshan (Peaceful Hill) Hall and Xiling (Spirit-Resting) Pagoda.

The Twenty-Four-Bridge Scenic Area

The Prospect Garden
(*Zhanyuan* 瞻园)

The Prospect Garden in Nanjing was used as a residence of a famous general in the early Ming Dynasty. In the Qing Dynasty, it was the site of a regional office, and Emperor Qianlong once stayed here. During the period of the Taiping Heavenly Kingdom (18951-1864), it was the residence of Yang Xiuqing (one of the leaders of the Kingdom) before it was burnt down. The garden was rebuilt twice in the second half of the 19th century in the Qing Dynasty. Renovated in 1960, the Prospect Garden is representative of classic Nanjing garden art and includes contemporary modern garden construction on a layout that retains the unique style of the Ming and Qing dynasties.

Newly established scenic area

A rockery built in the Qing Dynasty in southern area

The rockery in northern part maintains its Ming Dynasty style

The Balmy Garden
(*Xuyuan* 煦园)

The Balmy Garden in Nanjing is one of China's Historical Monuments and Cultural Relics under State Protection, first built in the early Ming Dynasty about 600 years ago. In 1647, the office of the governor-general was set up in the Balmy Garden, which later became part of the palace of the Taiping Heavenly Kingdom. Emperor Qianlong took it as an imperial garden during his second trip to the south in the Qing Dynasty. On New Year's Day 1912, Sun Yat-sen took the oath of office in the Balmy Garden as Provisional President of the Republic of China. In 1927, it became the presidential garden of the Kuomingtang (Nationalist Party). A marble boat on the south and a pavilion on the north echo each other from a distance, connected by a large body of water in the central area. The landscape arrangement of this long vase-shaped garden is most typical of ones south of the Yangtze River.

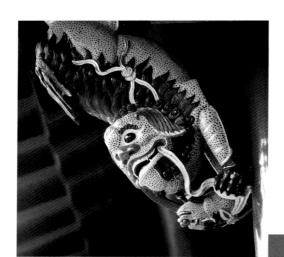

Decorations on the pillars of a corridor

A dragon wall (below) with a detail of the dragon's head (left)

The marble boat

The Mandarin Duck Pavilion in snow

Jinyuan Garden
(*Jinyuan* 近园)

Built in mid-19th century in the Qing Dynasty, Jinyuan Garden inside the Changzhou Hotel in Changzhou is a classical garden existing from the late Ming Dynasty style. Though it covers a small area, the garden has a complete layout with water and rockery, pavilions, halls, corridors, hills, paths, and a bridge all well arranged and set in a natural landscape of plants and bamboo grooves.

Wall of the Jinyuan Garden

Jianyi Pavilion

Decorative window

64

The Garden for Ease of Mind
(*Jichangyuan* 寄畅园)

The Garden for Ease of Mind in Wuxi in Jiangsu Province is one of the oldest and most complete classical gardens south of the Yangtze River. This garden was once a monastery in the Yuan Dynasty. Purchased by Qin Jin, a minister of war in Nanjing during the Ming Dynasty, it was expanded into a private garden. Following that, it was in the possession of a Qin family for over 400 years, the only example of a classical garden remaining in one family for so long. Covering an area of about 10,000 square meters, the Garden for Ease of Mind includes a corridor built over water in the east, trees and artificial hills in the west arranged to integrate artificial scenic sites with nature in a way characteristic of Chinese traditional gardening art.

Borrowing from the views of the Huishan Hill

Landscape in the east of the garden

Lingering Garden
(*Liuyuan* 留园)

Built in 1593 and meticulously restored in 1954, Suzhou's Lingering Garden is one of the most famous classical gardens in China. The garden was originally constructed and owned by Xu Taishi, a minister of the Court of the Ming Dynasty. Later, the garden changed hands several times and was renovated and expanded in the Qing Dynasty. In the War of Resistance against Japan (1931-1945), the Kuomintang once used it as a stable. Today the garden features magnificent towers, pavilions and courtyards throughout four scenic areas arranged in the style of gardens south of the Yangtze River, acclaimed for epitomizing the art of garden design employing a combination of different courtyards.

Cloud Crowned Peak

67

Pavilion for Quiet Meditation

Mingse (Bright and Clear) Tower and Hanbi
(Green) Mountain Villa along the water

Mandarin Duck Hall

Lion Grove Garden
(*Shizilin* 狮子林)

Lion Grove Garden is one of the most famous gardens of Suzhou. Originally built as a temple garden in 1342 by the Buddhist master Tianru (who named it "Lion Grove"), it was not until 1736 in the Qing Dynasty that the garden was separated from the temple to become a private one. Surrounded by high walls and laid out on a rectangular covering 1.2 hectares, Lion Grove Garden is particularly known for its rockworks and high hills created to form a natural landscape that surrounds a traditional arrangement of buildings and corridors.

Yanyu (Swallow's Blessing) Hall

A view through a doorway

Waterside corridor

Nine-Lion Summit

Pleasure Garden
(*Yiyuan* 怡园)

Built in the late Qing Dynasty, Suzhou's Pleasure Garden is typical of the private gardens in regions south of the Yangtze River, combining a residence and ancestral temple. Starting in 1872, a court administrator of Ningshao, Zhejiang, spent 0.2 million taels of silver over seven years to build up the garden. Pleasure Garden borrows features from other excellent gardens: The covered corridor resembles the one in the Surging Waves Pavilion; the pools, those of Master-of-Nets Garden; the rockery, that of Mountain Villa with Embracing Beauty; the caves, those of Lion Grove; and Huafang (Brightly-painted Pleasure Boat) Study and Mianbi (Facing the Wall) Pavilion resemble similar structures in the Humble Administrator's Garden.

Ouxiang (Fragrant Lotus Root) Waterside Pavilion

Cloud Wall and the door to a cave

Humble Administrator's Garden
(*Zhuozhengyuan* 拙政园)

The Humble Administrator's Garden at 4.8 hectares is the biggest classical garden in Suzhou. Built in the Ming Dynasty but with elements that date back to the Yuan Dynasty, the garden is typical of Ming and Qing dynasty gardens south of the Yangtze River, with buildings, trees and other landscaping arranged around water and bamboo. Rebuilt several times over the years, the Humble Administrator's Garden includes three separate areas— eastern, middle and western. The middle area expresses the essence of the garden as captured in the poetic line:

"A place of eternal spring, with endless scenery, half-revealed." A central pond here covers two-fifths of the area. On the southern bank are halls, rooms and pavilions of varied design, linked by covered corridors and winding bridges. The western area also has a central pond, to the west of which is a winding stream leading to residential area. The covered corridor along this stream can be considered a masterpiece of such structures found south of the Yangtze River.

Yuanxiang (Fragrance from a Distance) Hall

73

Xiangzhou (Fragrant Island)

Doorways and decorative windows of various forms

Xiao Feihong (Little Flying Rainbow)

Waterside corridor

The middle scenic area

Mountain Villa with Embracing Beauty
(*Huanxiu Shanzhuang* 环秀山庄)

The rockwork at Mountain Villa with Embracing Beauty is considered outstanding among Suzhou's gardens. With lakes, stones and rockeries that cover an area of just 330 square meters, the Mountain Villa has a design that features its hills, not its water. A lake serves as a counterpoint to the rockwork that, it is said in China, "has no equal in regions south of the Yangtze River." In the Five Dynasties (907-979), the garden was owned by Guangling Lord in Wuyue State. In the Song Dynasty, it was first a music garden, then an academy of classical learning, later a temple—Jingde Temple—and still later as a yamen, a government office in feudal China. In the Ming Dynasty it was a private residence. The garden began to take its present shape as a private garden in the Qing Dynasty.

Garden of Cultivation
(*Yipu* 艺圃)

The Garden of Cultivation in Suzhou once was a herb garden of the great-grandson of Wen Zhengming, a Ming Dynasty scholar. The garden centers on a pond, to the south of which is a relatively large-scale rockery; and to the west, an archway leading to a secluded courtyard. The scenery in the garden is open and natural, retaining the layout of Ming Dynasty gardens.

Ruyu (Minnow) Pavilion
and a rockery

Moon archway

The pond in the center of garden

77

Couple's Garden Retreat
(*Ouyuan* 耦园)

Located at Xiaoxinqiao Lane in eastern Suzhou, the Couple's Garden Retreat is surrounded by water on three sides and land on one side, covering an area of 7,333 square meters. In the center of the garden is a house with a garden on its east and a garden on its west, an arrangement that helped inspire its name. The east garden was built by the prefect of Baoning in the early Qing Dynasty. Later in the Qing Dynasty, the governor of Anhui Province purchased the complex and added the west garden. Couple's Garden Retreat contains buildings with courtyards and corridors, towers, rockeries, pools, pavilions, and trees. The theme of a couple's seclusion can be found widely in inscriptions on steles, plaques and couplets.

A canal north of the Couple's Garden Retreat

Zaijiu Wine-Storage Hall in the eastern garden

Prineiple scenery of the eastern garden

Viewing the rockworks in the
pool over a window

Rockeries and covered corridor
in the western garden

Master-of-Nets Garden
(*Wangshiyuan* 网师园)

Master-of-Nets Garden in the southeast of Suzhou is famous for its intact houses and courtyards, small size (a total area of only 0.6 of a hectare) but elegant style, particularly in its water landscapes. A house in the east of the garden is typical of those residences of Suzhou's court officials. Master-of-Nets Garden was built on the site of "Wanjuan (Ten Thousand Volume) Hall" of Shi Zhengzhi, a vice minister of the Ministry of Personnel in the Southern Song Dynasty (1127-1279). In the Qing Dynasty, the garden passed through the hands of officials and wealthy businessmen during the successive reigns of several emperors. In 1930s, prominent artists like Zhang Daqian, Zhang Shanzi and Ye Gongchuo lived in the garden.

Gable wall of Jixiu (Picking Beautiful Scenery) Tower mirroring in the water

Courtyard of Dianchun (Deep Spring) Study

Sheya (Shooting at Ducks) Corridor

Ming (Bright) Veranda

Principal scene of the garden

Gate built with carved bricks

Wanjuan (Ten Thousand Volume) Hall

Decorative windows

Surging Waves Pavilion
(Canglangting 沧浪亭)

The Surging Waves Pavilion has the longest history of all the gardens in Suzhou, a history that also exerted considerable influence through its purchase as a retreat by Su Shunqin, a demoted official in the Northern Song Dynasty 1,000 years ago. Subsequently, gardens became places of interest for those like Su who had been disappointed in public life, and names for gardens appeared such as "Humble Administrator's Garden" and "Retreat and Reflection Garden." In earlier dynasties, the garden served as the residence of a military commissioner of the Middle Wu Army in Wuyue Kingdom in the Five Dynasties; later as the residence of Han Shizhong, a famous general of the Southern Song Dynasty; and as a monastery in the Yuan Dynasty. In 1873 in the Qing Dynasty, a provincial governor renovated Surging Waves Pavilion and added Mingdao Hall. With all the changes over its long history, the garden no longer has the appearance of the Song Dynasty, but retains the basic layout of that time. The buildings here are characterized by simple architecture, and the latticework in 108 varied forms is considered the best of all such work in Suzhou.

Making use of space for miniature landscape designs

Interior decoration is a feature of Suzhou gardens.

84

Entrance to the Surging Waves Pavilion

The Thatched Abode of Seclusion and Meditation

Retreat an Reflection Garden
(*Tuisiyuan* 退思园)

Retreat and Reflection Garden is an important scenic area of the Taihu Lake Scenic Area in Wujiang City of southern Jiangsu. It was built in 1885 in the Qing Dynasty by Ren Lansheng, a military defense official, after he retired to his hometown. The west-east layout caused by limitations in the terrain is the only example of such a layout in gardens south of the Yangtze River. Houses with courtyards, a tea pavilion, principal hall, a double corri-

dor and towers in the western and middle areas are featured with camphor trees forming a canopy in the courtyards. The flower garden in the east is the most prominent place of the whole site, covering more than half of its area. The garden is noble and complete in all its elements, centering on a lotus pond surrounded by some scenic spots.

The principal scenery

Yuyuan Garden
(*Yuyuan* 豫园)

Located in the old city area in southern Shanghai by the Huangpu River, Yuyuan Garden was owned by Pan Chongrui, administration commissioner of Sichuan Province, after it was built in 1559 in the Ming Dynasty. Over the years in the late Ming Dynasty it was built and rebuilt, and some of its buildings even became shops and a school. Starting in 1956, some 2 hectares were restored in a garden that features rockeries, caves, and gullies. The Lotus Pond, Zigzag Bridge and Pavilion in the Pond outside the garden used to be part of the garden.

Yangshan (Looking Up at the Mountain) Hall

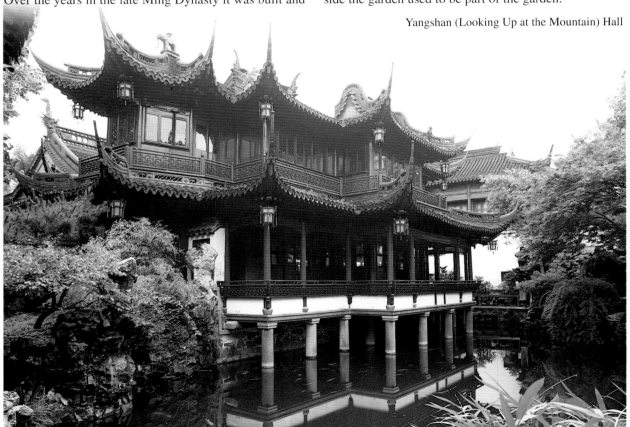

Dianchun (Hint of Spring) Hall

Sightseeing in rain

Kuai Tower and rockeries in the garden

The Pavilion in the Pond and the Zigzag
Bridge outside the garden

A big stage

Scenery in the
garden

91

Ancient Ripples Garden
(*Guyiyuan*古漪园)

Built by an assistant prefect of Song County in Henan Province during the Ming Dynasty, the six-hectare Guyi garden was restored in 1958. Bamboo Twigs Hill is the highest point in the garden with a square pavilion that features a geometric dome painted with nine flying dragons in clouds. The northeastern corner of the dome was purposely made incomplete to commemorate the suffering caused the nation by the September 18, 1931 Japanese invasion of northeast China. In the center of the garden is the Pool for Playing with Geese. Beside the pool stands a pavilion with a plaque inscribed in the handwriting of Zhu Xi, a philosopher in the Song Dynasty (960-1279). Also by the pool is a small, painted marble boat. The two light-gray stone pillars inscribed with scriptures, together with Putong (Great Harmony) Stone Pagoda in the Lotus Pond, are 1,000-year-old cultural relics.

Spring in the garden

The marble boat

Garden of Liu Manor
(*Liuzhuang* 刘庄)

Enjoying the reputation as "the greatest garden along the West Lake," the Garden of Liu Manor in Hangzhou includes the most magnificent of the manors and villas along the Su Causeway of the West Lake. The garden was built at the foot of Dingjia Mountain in 1905 according to the style of the Liu Garden in Guangdong, representing a style found in Guangdong and Guangxi areas. The designer of the garden planted rare flowers and trees; set up pavilions, halls, towers and terraces; developed woods and springs; constructed long corridors and winding bridges; and purchased precious furniture, antiques, scrolls and paintings. With this refined atmosphere, Liu Manor came to be regarded as "The Pearl of West Lake." Renovated in 1954, the Garden of Liu Manor includes five private gardens: Han Manor, Yang Manor, Kang Manor, Fan Manor and Liu Manor.

In front of the arch over the entrance to the Garden of Liu Manor flows a river through a stand of dense green woods. Inside—to the right of a stand of towering pines, magnolia and maple trees—is an island with 14 hardy and old Japanese black pines standing beside a stele inscribed "Evergreen Pine Island." A winding bridge links the two ends of the island. The main building in the garden features long corridors with views to the Su Causeway and the West Lake. As an official state residence, Garden of Liu Manor has welcomed heads of states such as President Richard M. Nixon of the United States and President Josip Broz Tito of the former Yugoslavia.

Guozhuang Garden

(*Guozhuang* 郭庄)

Among the gardens of the West Lake in Hangzhou, Guozhuang Garden is the most typical of the classical private gardens found south of the Yangtze River. Renovated to its original layout and area and opened to the public in 1991, the garden was built on the west bank of West Lake by Song Duanpu, a silk merchant in the mid-19th century during the Qing Dynasty. It is located be- side the Crouching Dragon Bridge, south of the attraction "Lotus in the Breeze in the Curved Courtyard." The Guozhuang Garden is divided into a residential and a garden area. The garden area is arranged with a pool as the center surrounded by pavilions, chambers, corridors and rockeries.

The Tower of Viewing Su

Each part of this corridor frames a distinct and different view.

The Hall of Fragrant Snow Heralding Spring

The Chamber of Literary Prosperity
(*Wenlange* 文澜阁)

The Chamber of Literary Prosperity is one of seven chambers recorded in *The Complete Library of Four Branches of Books* kept by the Qing imperial court. Built in 1782, the chamber was destroyed in the mid-19th century and later restored in 1880 under the Qing Emperor Guangxu. As an imitation of the Chamber of Tianyi (Heavenly Harmony) in Ningbo, the Chamber of Literary Prosperity has in front of it a square pool. In the pool stands a rare rock formation named "The Immortal Hill," considered a masterpiece among the rockworks of Hangzhou's West Lake.

The Former Residence of Hu Xueyan
(*Hu Xueyuan Guju* 胡雪岩故居)

One of the famous gardens south of the Yangtze River, the Former Residence of Hu Xueyan in Hangzhou was built in 1872 by Hu Xueyan, the founder of Hu Qingyu's Drug Store at the cost of 100,000 taels of silver. The rockwork was created by well-known craftsmen like Wei Shifu according to the design of the rock landscape artist Yin Zhi. This 0.72-hectare garden is located in Hangzhou on Yuanbao Street opposite the Drum Tower.

Carved windows
and doors

Exquisite rosewood
sedan chairs

The Hall of Bathing in Autumn

Principal scenery of the garden

Fond Abode Garden
(*Keyuan* 可园)

Keyuan or Fond Abode Garden is one of the best-known gardens in Central Guangdong Province with landscape architecture that sets buildings in harmonious relationship with hills, ponds, flowers and trees. Originally the residence of a Mao family, the residence was purchased in 1850 by an official named Zhang Jingxiu, who then built the garden on an area of only 0.2 hectare.

A terrace in the garden

Courtyard

"Watching Fish on Ke Lake"

Kelou Tower

The Garden of Pure Sunshine
(Qinghuiyuan 清晖园)

The Garden of Pure Sunshine in Daliang County, built in the Qing Dynasty in the late 18th century, is one of the best gardens in Guangdong Province. Covering an area of 0.3 hectares, the garden in its central part has a pavilion, the Time-Cherishing Study, Lion Hill and precious flowers and trees. The owner lived in a cottage in a bamboo garden in the northern part while the southern part features water. Small as it is, the garden contains many scenic spots that incorporate Lingnan (the area covering Guangdong and Guangxi provinces) gardening art with Chinese classical gardening art.

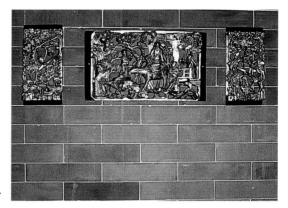

Decoration on the wall of the corridor

Corridor outside the Thatch-Roofed Cottage of Green Stream

102

One can have a bird's-eye view of the whole garden from the watchtower—a feature of Lingnan-styled gardens.

Indoor decorations highlight the gardening art of Lingnan.

A scene of the garden

The Cottage in the Shade

(*Yuyin Shanfang* 余荫山房)

Covering an area of only 2000 square meters, the Cottage in the Shade with its waterside pavilions, terraces, rockeries and flowers reflects the best of the gardening arts of Beijing, Suzhou and Lingnan. Located in Nancun Village, Panyu City in Guangdong Province, it was considered one of the four famous gardens during the period from the mid-19th century to 1919 in the province. (The other three: Keyuan Garden in Dongguan, Liang Garden in Foshan, and the Garden of Pure Sunshine in Shunde.) It was the private garden of a *juren* (a successful candidate in the imperial examinations at the provincial level) in the mid-19th century.

Looking east from the octagonal pavilion

Entrace to the Cottage in the Shade

104

Exquisite brick carvings

Chamber by the Pool

Having a sister means you
are never alone in the world.

To Donna

Love You Always,
From
Jill

May 11ᵀᴴ, 2004

Happy 45ᵀᴴ Birthday

Sisters

Picture credits:

Front cover (inset): **Orion Press/Natural Selections**
Book jacket illustrated by **Robin Moro.**
Bridgeman Art Library: *Song for Summer* by Allan R. Banks/Elgin Court Designs Ltd., London; © 2003 Artists Rights Society
(ARS), New York/ADAGP, Paris/*Two Sisters* by Marie Laurencin/Galerie Daniel Malingue, Paris; *Two Sisters* by Bessie Macni-
col/Ferens Art Gallery, Hull City Museums and Art Galleries; *Children at the Basin* by Berthe Morisot/Musee Marmottan, Paris;
Denise Hilton Campbell; J.C. Carton/Bruce Coleman, Inc.; © **Corbis:** Archivo Iconografico,.S.A: Christie's Images; Philadel-
phia Museum of Art; **Michael Jaroszko; Rosanne Kaloustian; Orion Press/Natural Selection; Joyce Shelton; SuperStock:**
Bridgeman Art Library, London; Hyacinth Manning-Carner; David David Gallery; Musee D'Orsay, Paris/Giraudon

Contributing writers:

June Eaton, Lain Chroust Ehmann, Jan Goldberg, Jennifer Ouellette, June Stevenson
Other quotes compiled by Joan Loshek.

Acknowledgments:

Publications International, Ltd., has made every effort to locate the owners of all copyrighted material to obtain permission to use the
selections that appear in this book. Any errors or omissions are unintentional; corrections, if necessary, will be made in future editions.
Excerpt by Iyanla Vanzant taken from *Sisterfriends: Portraits of Sisterly Love* by Julia Chance. Copyright © 2001 by Julia Chance.
Reprinted by permission of Pocket Books, a division of Simon & Schuster.
Excerpt by The Reverend Shaheerah Stephens taken from *Sisterfriends: Portraits of Sisterly Love* by Julia Chance. Copyright © 2001
by Julia Chance. Reprinted by permission of Pocket Books, a division of Simon & Schuster.
Excerpt from "Sisters" by Irving Berlin. Copyright © 1953 by Irving Berlin. Copyright renewed. International copyright secured.
All rights reserved. Reprinted by permission.

You know full as well as I do the value of sisters' affections
to each other; there is nothing like it in this world.

CHARLOTTE BRONTË

Sister is a word I hold in
my heart. It is a precious
reminder of who I am
and where my roots are;
a link between the
present and the past.

You are more than my sister. You
are friend, companion, keeper of
memories, and a reservoir of who
I was and what I am becoming.

A sister is someone who saw you through your "ugly duckling" days of braces and pimples and still believes you've always been a swan.

My sister: When we were young, you were the enemy I had to love. Now that we're older, you're the friend I love to have.

You and I don't need
a lot of words. Just say,
"Remember when . . . ," and
we dissolve into giggles,
sighs, and sometimes tears.
Isn't it great being sisters?

Sister is such a lovely word on the tongue. I savor each cherished memory it brings to mind.

Even when the miles separate us, we are close in thought.

Having a sister is better than having a therapist.

*L*ooking at you is like looking in a mirror. I see my childhood reflected, my growing years. All I have been and all I am today is there in your eyes.

When I think about scraped
knees and bruised hearts I
think about you. When I
crave ice cream sundaes and
cotton candy, I remember
the times we shared. They
have a place all
their own in
treasure chest
of memories.

You and I—we are like buds on a rose bush. We've always been there for each other: holding hands, linking arms, hugging each other closely. We have a closeness that the world can never take from us.

We can be so
different and yet
feel so alike.
Accepting each
other for who we
are is what makes
our relationship
so special.

Through years of practice, sisters learn to dance
without stepping on each others' toes.

Just as good friends can become the
sisters we never had, sisters can become
the best friends we've always longed for.

Sisters are like flowers grown in
the same soil; each has identical
roots but offers a unique beauty
to the garden.

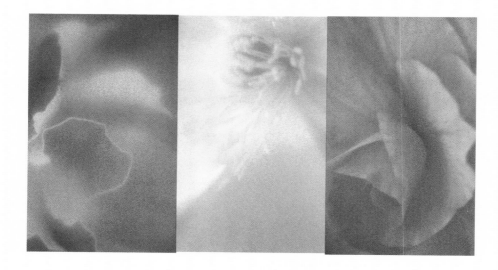

$\mathcal{M}$My sister taught me everything I really need to know, and she was only in sixth grade at the time.

LINDA SUNSHINE, *MOM LOVES ME BEST (AND OTHER LIES YOU TOLD YOUR SISTER)*

Sisters are like mirrors reflecting
the best of ourselves; in their
eyes, we can see all that we are
and all that we can be.

Sisters are nuts from the same family tree.

Sisters see beyond the surface to the feelings we hide from all but those who know us best. They listen to our hearts not our words.

Talking with your sister is like paging through a scrapbook of your life. All the memories are there, just waiting to be relived and rediscovered.

Growing up with my sister is my most treasured childhood memory.

To have a sister you can call "friend" is quite
possibly life's greatest gift.

Sisters are lifelines for one another.

IYANLA VANZANT, "IYANLA VANZANT AND SHAHEERAH STEPHENS: SISTER SPIRIT,"

SISTERFRIENDS: PORTRAITS OF SISTERLY LOVE

Looking back on the name calling, hair pulling, and wrestling matches, there is just one thing to say: "You started it!"

As sisters grow older their
relationship changes—they go from
enemies to friends.

A sister knows all your deep dark secrets like your true bikini size, your obsession with those ugly plaid pants, and even your most annoying habits— but she still wouldn't change a thing about you.

It is a fortunate person who is able to say,
"I have a sister."

When you were a kid, your sister got you IN trouble: As an adult, your sister gets you OUT of trouble.

Some friends only surround you when times are good, but a sister is there to pick you up when everyone else walks away.

You can fool some of the people all of the time,
and all of the people some of the time,
but you can never fool your sister.

Sisters are the best reminder of the little kid
hiding deep inside all of us.

A sister is someone who comes over and helps you cook and clean for a party she isn't even invited to.

Lord help the mister
Who comes between me
and my sister,
and Lord help the sister
Who comes between me
and my man.

Irving Berlin, "Sisters"

When you trip along the path of life, your
sister is the first to dry your tears, dust
you off, and carry you home.

My sister is a blessing. Without her, who else could I have blamed when something got broken?

I am so thankful for my best friend. Because not only
is she my most treasured friend, she is my sister.

Remember all those times I made you cry when we were kids? And when I got you in trouble for things I did? Or when I told on you because you didn't do your chores? Well, I really had your best interests at heart. I was simply trying to make you a stronger person. Don't thank me—that's what sisters are for.

A sister is sombody who loves,
understands, and wants the very
best for you. They believe in you
even when you don't always
believe in yourself.

THE REVEREND SHAHEERAH STEPHENS, "IYANLA

VANZANT AND SHAHEERAH STEPHENS: SISTER SPIRIT,"

SISTERFRIENDS: PORTRAITS OF SISTERLY LOVE

I can't even count how many fights started because,
"She's looking at me!" Now I only wish we had that
much time to spend together.

It doesn't matter how the rest of your life is going—if your sister likes you, you're doing something right!

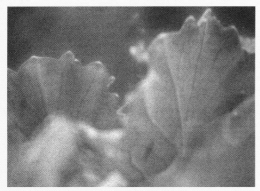

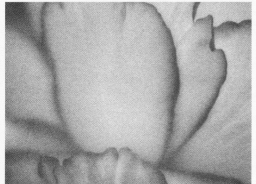

If the length of a friendship is the measure of its strength, I can have no better friend than my sister.

Sisters love us as much for the little girls we once were
as for the women we've become.

Sisters are like good
insurance policies.
Even when you don't
need them, you get
comfort just knowing
they're there.

Sisterhood is made of layer upon layer of little memories—
dinnertime giggles, secrets told by the bedroom nightlight, never-
ending hours in the backseat of the car on long summer road trips.
These moments create a collage that others may admire but only
the two of us really understand.

Some sweet slices of your life can
only be shared with your sister.

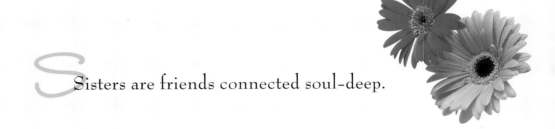

Sisters are friends connected soul-deep.

For there is no friend like a sister.

CHRISTINA ROSETTI

No matter how bad things got when I was growing up, I knew I could depend on you to say those three magic words: "I'm telling Mom!"

I'm always amazed when I see you now—you're an accomplished adult. But I still see the twinkle in your eyes of the sister who involved me in so much mischief! Thank heavens she's still there—and still sometimes involves me in mischief!

Sisters offer a voice of reason as well as a voice of inspiration. When things are going well, sisters can remind you to keep your feet on the ground. When things are tough, they can remind you to aim for the stars.

Jobs, boyfriends, hemlines, and hairstyles may come and go, but a sister lasts forever.

No problem is so
bad and no joy is
so great that it
can't be made
better by sharing it
with a sister.

A sister's smile can brighten
even the most cloudy day.

My favorite person to laugh, cry, and gossip with is my sister.

I Love You So Much Joanne.
Love, Jill